W9-ARN-186

WITHDRAWN

FRANKLIN PARK PUBLIC LIBRARY
FRANKLIN PARK, IL.

Each borrower is held responsible for all library
material drawn on his card and for fines accruing on
the same. No material will be issued until such fine
has been paid.

All injuries to library material beyond reasonable
wear and all losses shall be made good to the
satisfaction of the Librarian

Replacement costs will be
billed after 45 days overdue.

WRESTLING SUPERST★RS

JOHN CENA

BY BLAKE MARKEGARD

EPIC

BELLWETHER MEDIA • MINNEAPOLIS, MN

EPIC BOOKS are no ordinary books. They burst with intense action, high-speed heroics, and shadows of the unknown. Are you ready for an Epic adventure?

This edition first published in 2015 by Bellwether Media, Inc.

No part of this publication may be reproduced in whole or in part without written permission of the publisher. For information regarding permission, write to Bellwether Media, Inc., Attention: Permissions Department, 5357 Penn Avenue South, Minneapolis, MN 55419.

Library of Congress Cataloging-in-Publication Data

Markegard, Blake.
  John Cena / by Blake Markegard.
    pages cm. – (Epic: Wrestling Superstars)
  Includes bibliographical references and index.
  Summary: "Engaging images accompany information about John Cena. The combination of high-interest subject matter and light text is intended for students in grades 2 through 7"– Provided by publisher.
  ISBN 978-1-62617-141-1 (hardcover : alk. paper)
  1. Cena, John–Juvenile literature. 2. Wrestlers–United States–Biography–Juvenile literature. 3. Motion picture actors and actresses–United States–Biography–Juvenile literature. I. Title.
  GV1196.C46M37 2014
  796.812092–dc23
  [B]
                        2014011772

Printed in the United States of America, North Mankato, MN.

TABLE OF CONTENTS

WARNING!

The wrestling moves used in this book are performed by professionals.
Do not attempt to reenact any of the moves performed in this book.

THE DEBUT

Kurt Angle invites new challengers to wrestle. John Cena steps out of the locker room. He will be **ruthless** to the wrestling champion.

KURT
ANGLE

Cena tackles Angle. He escapes **pins**
and tries to make his own. In the end,
Angle gets the win. But Cena impresses
fans with his **debut**.

WHO IS JOHN CENA?

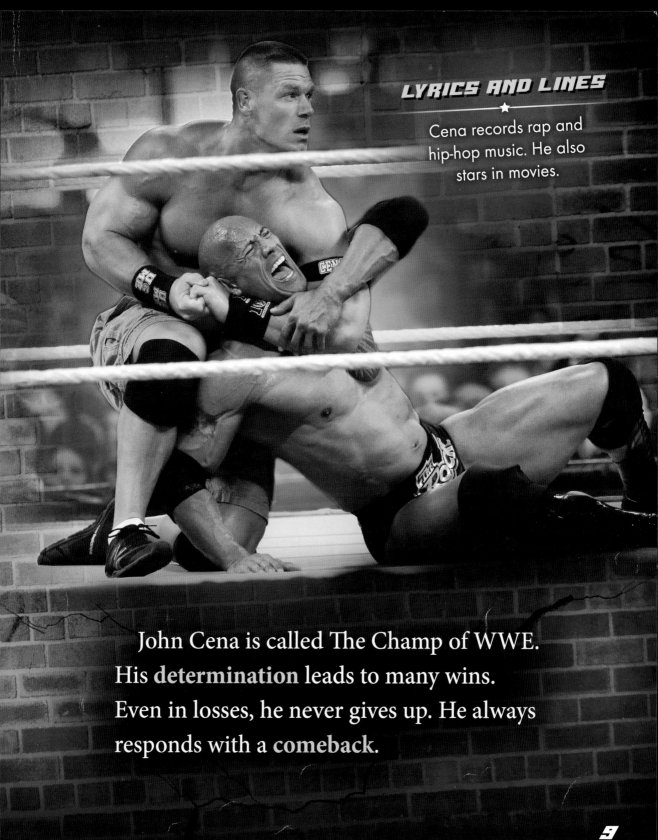

Cena records rap and hip-hop music. He also stars in movies.

John Cena is called The Champ of WWE. His **determination** leads to many wins. Even in losses, he never gives up. He always responds with a **comeback**.

LIFE BEFORE WWE

As a teen, Cena lifted weights to get bigger. He went on to play football in college. He also graduated with a degree in **exercise physiology**.

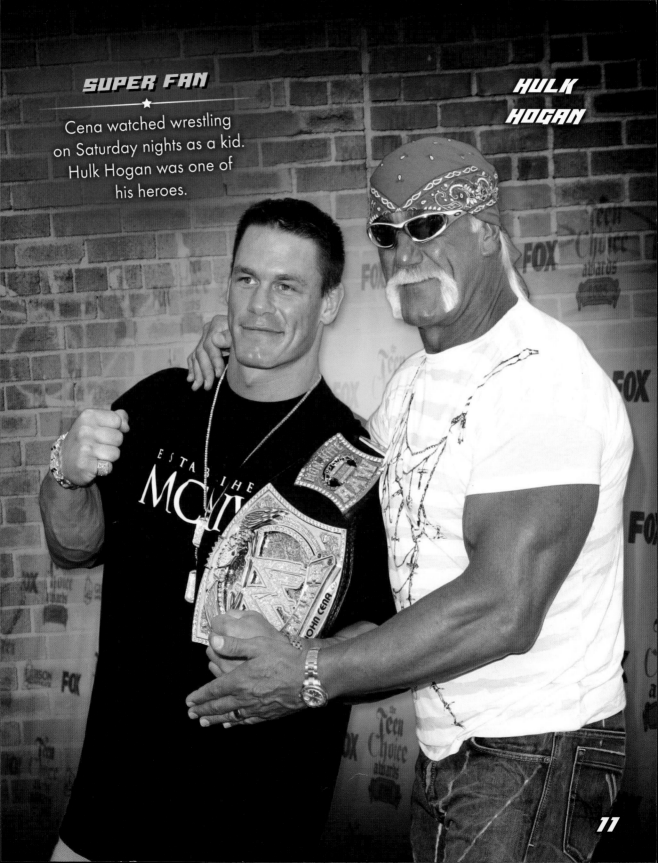

Cena watched wrestling on Saturday nights as a kid. Hulk Hogan was one of his heroes.

HULK HOGAN

Cena became a **bodybuilder** after college. To make money, he cleaned a gym. Members there encouraged him to wrestle. Soon Cena competed as The Prototype.

A WWE SUPERSTAR

STAR PROFILE

WRESTLING NAME: John Cena

REAL NAME: John Felix Anthony Cena

BIRTHDATE: April 23, 1977

HOMETOWN: West Newbury, Massachusetts

HEIGHT: 6 feet, 1 inch (1.9 meters)

WEIGHT: 251 pounds (114 kilograms)

WWE DEBUT: 2002

FINISHING MOVE: Attitude Adjustment

A developmental contract led to a WWE debut in 2002. Fans embraced Cena as a face early on. Cena had a hip-hop style. He freestyle rapped to challenge opponents.

In 2004, Cena became the United States Champion. Twenty more championship wins have followed since. Few WWE wrestlers have **reigned** for more total days.

MR. CASUAL
★
Cena usually wrestles in
baggy jean shorts.

WINNING MOVES

Cena often gives his opponents an Attitude Adjustment in the ring. He puts a wrestler on his shoulders for this **finishing move**. Then he throws him onto the mat.

ATTITUDE
ADJUSTMENT

STEP OVER
TOEHOLD FACELOCK
(STF)

The Stepover Toehold Facelock (STF) is another **signature move**. Cena sits on top of a wrestler's back. He locks his opponent's ankle and head. Then he gives a painful pull.

GLOSSARY

bodybuilder—a person who works to increase the strength and size of his or her muscles

comeback—a return to success

debut—first official appearance

determination—the drive to try to achieve

developmental contract—an agreement between WWE and a wrestler; WWE promises to train the wrestler in smaller leagues.

exercise physiology—the study of exercise and the human body

face—a wrestler viewed as a hero

finishing move—a wrestling move that finishes off an opponent

pins—wrestling holds that end matches

prototype—a model that is copied or developed more

reigned—held champion standing

ruthless—mean

signature move—a move that a wrestler is famous for performing

TO LEARN MORE

At the Library

Black, Jake. *WWE General Manager's Handbook*. New York, N.Y.: Grosset & Dunlap, 2012.

Markegard, Blake. *Sheamus*. Minneapolis, Minn.: Bellwether Media, 2015.

West, Tracey. *Race to the Rumble*. New York, N.Y.: Grosset & Dunlap, 2011.

On the Web

Learning more about John Cena is as easy as 1, 2, 3.

1. Go to www.factsurfer.com.

2. Enter "John Cena" into the search box.

3. Click the "Surf" button and you will see a list of related web sites.

With factsurfer.com, finding more information is just a click away.

INDEX